Human Relations Protocol

Susan Louise Peterson

Human Relations Protocol
Susan Louise Peterson

COPYRIGHT

CONTENTS

PREFACE

J must confess to you that as I started writing ***Human Relations Protocol*** I took a different angle in examining what many people consider to be protocol. This book is not about procedural protocol and the exact methods to conduct a perfect meeting or plan a flawless ceremony. It is not about which person you introduce first at a seminar or social function. The book does not explore the perfect way to be polite and courtesy at a highly formal event. The book takes a fresh approach to examining protocol from a very personal human relations perspective. ***Human Relations Protocol*** is an exploration into the choices that professionals make in the workplace and the consequences of those choices. ***Human Relations Protocol*** has a goal of encouraging growth into more positive human relationships in the work environment.

PROLOGUE

On my journey from college graduation to finding my first professional job I ran into a series of unprofessional mishaps. My ambitious plan to send out hundreds of resumes and find the perfect job was often spoiled by unprofessional responses, discourteous remarks and staff who lacked a sense of human relations. It caused me as a job seeker to quickly get discouraged in a system filled with educated 'professional' people who lacked basic human relations skills. Over the years, I have thought a lot about those early personal experiences, the consequences of the professional's actions and ways professionals could become more in touch with the human relations side of the work world. I later became a school psychologist coordinating team members in multi-team assessments, conducting eligibility meetings and working with professionals and parents with varying opinions on a daily basis. This taught me to see the need for more training in the area of human relations. I wrote ***Human Relations Protocol*** as a practical guide for encouraging successful human relations choices in the professional world.

ACKNOWLEDGMENTS

I would like to thank the many professionals who have helped me to learn about caring, respect and showing goodwill toward others. Sometimes just a brief comment, a pat on the back and some reassurance during a difficult situation have helped ease the stress and allowed me to reflect on the more positive aspects of a situation. Your kindness will not be forgotten!

I want to thank my husband for his continual support of my writing career and his ongoing patience for being married to a writer. I would also like to thank my twin 'college bound' daughters who teach me new things everyday about the choices we make and the acceptance of others.

INTRODUCTION

The thing I love most about the human relations world is that it takes a very multidisciplinary approach to life. When I think of human relations in the work environment I see the importance of communication exchange, social interaction and a variety of psychological issues related to feelings, attitudes, choices and responses to each other. The area of choice is so important in the work environment because these choices all have consequences that impact the day to day operations and the human relationships the employees are building with one another and with customers. If more emphasis in the work world focused on human relations aspects, professionals would feel more valued and perhaps more willing to seek professional growth and gain fulfillment in their careers. I wrote **Human Relations Protocol** to emphasize why human relations messages are important and how these principles can make the professional work environment a more positive and enriching place.

CHAPTER 1

THE DEFINITION OF HUMAN RELATIONS PROTOCOL

DEFINITION

Human Relations Protocol refers to the manner that professionals behave and the choices that professionals make as they communicate with others in various occupation and social settings.

THE RATIONALE BEHIND HUMAN RELATIONS PROTOCOL

Human Relations Protocol is concerned with:

improving the employee-employer relationship

enhancing customer relations

increasing business and professional opportunities

cultivating partnerships and collaborative relationships

heightening the image of organizations, corporations and businesses

gaining a personal fulfillment in one's career or occupation

HUMAN RELATIONS PROTOCOL ISSUES

Human Relations Protocol involves the following issues:

how people respond and react toward others

valuing the time of people in professional settings

showing respect for others in professional situations

acknowledging confidential issues in the professional arena

examining the attitude professionals have toward other people in the workplace

expressing gratitude to others in the work environment

closing out and completing projects and tasks started by the professional

seeking personal growth through professional relationships in the workplace

CHOICES OF
HUMAN RELATIONS PROTOCOL

RESPONSE CHOICES

TIME CHOICES

HUMAN RELATIONS CHOICES

COMPLETION CHOICES

EXAMPLES OF HUMAN RELATIONS PROTOCOL CHOICES

RESPONSE CHOICES

Responding with no response, delayed response, lack of action response, incorrect response, or appropriate response

TIME CHOICES

Making informal and formal time choices or casual and urgent time choices

HUMAN RELATIONS CHOICES

Responding with confidentiality choices, respect choices, attitude choices or motivation choices

COMPLETION CHOICES

Making gratitude choices, closure choices, or personal growth choices

KEY POINTS TO HUMAN RELATIONS PROTOCOL

Human Relations Protocol includes the following points:

identifying how our responses and actions make other people feel

examining the attitudes of workers and professional staff toward colleagues and the general public

cultivating positive relationships with customers, colleagues and others in the work environment

fulfilling jobs or task requirements and expectations

exhibiting a positive self image and confidence about work and responsibilities

WHY DO WE NEED A HUMAN RELATIONS PROTOCOL?

A human relations protocol is needed to provide a positive work environment.

A human relations protocol is needed for employees to show a healthy respect for each other.

A human relations protocol is needed so professionals will interact with each other in a considerate manner.

A human relations protocol is needed to keep work projects and activities running on a timely schedule.

A human relations protocol is needed to give positive responses and acknowledgments to others in the work environment.

HOW PROFESSIONAL PROTOCOL IS IMPORTANT TO HUMAN RELATIONS

Professional protocol can show many things that are important in human relations.

HUMAN RELATIONS PROTOCOL SHOWS THE PROFESSIONAL'S:

Goodwill

Caring

Concern

Respect

Contributions

Values

Confidence

Image

Genuineness

Sincerity

Motivation

Priorities

Trustworthiness

HUMAN RELATIONS PROTOCOL IS ABOUT

BEHAVIORS PEOPLE EXHIBIT

CHOICES PEOPLE MAKE

PRINCIPLES PEOPLE ESTABLISH

CHAPTER 2

RESPONSE CHOICES

Response choices are an important part of human relations protocol. Professionals are responding to many verbal and written requests by others during a workday. The response given by the professional communicates an image of that person and the corporation that he or she is representing at the time. There are basically five types of responses to a request:

NO RESPONSE

DELAYED RESPONSE

LACK OF ACTION RESPONSE

INCORRECT RESPONSE

APPROPRIATE RESPONSE

Each type of response has consequences for the professional. Response choice is important because it is a reflection of a business or organization. It is also an action that impacts the feelings of customers and individuals. These people will make their future decisions on the basis of the response choice of the professional.

TYPES OF RESPONSE CHOICES

NO RESPONSE
Professionals who give no response to requests from other individuals.

DELAYED RESPONSE
Professionals respond to requests with slow or delayed reply.

LACK OF ACTION RESPONSE
Professionals who make agreements or promises to a request and do not carry through on their promises and actions.

INCORRECT RESPONSE
Professionals respond to requests by providing inaccurate information or giving out wrong details.

APPROPRIATE RESPONSE
Professionals respond to requests by others in a prompt and courteous way with accurate information.

EXAMPLES OF NO RESPONSE

A woman had a question about some charges at a doctor's office where she had recently had an appointment. The woman called the doctor's office on Friday and asked to speak to the person in charge of the billing department. She was informed by the receptionist that the billing department manager did not work on Fridays and Mondays. The following Tuesday the woman called and asked to speak to the billing manager who was not available. The woman left a message, but her phone call was not returned. She called the doctor's office several more times on the following week and the phone calls were never returned. The woman wrote a detailed letter to the billing manager and asked for an itemized list of the office charges and insurance payment. There was never a response to the woman's written or oral request.

A man writes a detailed letter to a cleaning company complaining about the poor service he had received from workers cleaning his office building. The company did not answer his complaint letter or give a follow-up call to clarify or respond to these concerns.

A steering committee needs facts and statistics from an office to prepare a grant proposal. The office manager does not take the time to look up the information and does not provide it to the committee by the deadline date.

TYPES OF NO RESPONSE

REFUSING TO RETURN PHONE CALLS

UNWILLING TO PASS MESSAGES TO APPROPRIATE INDIVIDUALS

IGNORING REQUESTS FOR ADDITIONAL INFORMATION

BRUSHING OFF AN INVITATION

DECLINING TO PROVIDE NEEDED FACTS

UNWILLING TO CONSIDER OFFERS OR REQUESTS

WITHDRAWING DOCUMENTS FROM CERTAIN INDIVIDUALS

REFUSING TO GIVE REASONS WHY PROJECTS ARE REJECTED

WITHHOLDING IMPORTANT DOCUMENTS

REFUSING TO ANSWER LETTERS AND COMPLAINTS

CONSEQUENCES OF NO RESPONSE

Individuals get suspicious of business practices.

Customers have apprehension about the company.

People think the company is covering up a wrongdoing.

There is a mistrust of company employees.

Customers question the company procedures.

Customers become skeptics of how complaints are handled by the company.

The company is suspected of having problems or management trouble.

A trust is broken between the business and the customer.

There is doubt about company policies.

The customers feel the company does not value their business.

EXAMPLES OF DELAYED RESPONSE

A potential customer calls a business to compare prices of computers. The salesperson is busy and does not return the customer's call for two weeks.

A budding first time author mails a manuscript to a book editor to be considered for publication. The editor piles it in a stack and does not return a response until a year later.

A school does not supply the needed information requested from a foundation by the grant proposal deadline date. The grant proposal is not considered with the other applications and the school's funding may be in jeopardy.

Two companies are vying for the same contract. One company has everything completed before the deadline and in an efficient manner. The other company is constantly making excuses for late paperwork and is requesting extensions for each deadline. Which company do you think will make a more favorable impression when the contract is considered?

A client specifically requests the maid service to clean his house at 8 AM every Wednesday morning. The maid service does not show up at 8 AM. The client receives a call at 10 AM that the maid services will be late.

TYPES OF DELAYED RESPONSE

MAKING EXCUSES FOR A SLOW REPLY

PUTTING ITEMS ON HOLD FOR LONG PERIODS OF TIME

POSTPONING COMMITTEE MEETINGS WITHOUT REASON

RUNNING BEHIND ON A PROJECT BECAUSE OF UNCOMPLETED WORK

SLOW TO RETURN IMPORTANT MESSAGES

TAKING LONGER THAN USUAL TO COMPLETE TASKS

HOLDING UP A PROJECT BECAUSE OTHER THINGS ARE IN THE WAY

LETTING A PROJECT DELAY FOR A LONG TIME

PUTTING OFF AN ANSWER BECAUSE THE REQUEST DOES NOT SEEM IMPORTANT

PROCRASTINATING REPORTS UNTIL AFTER THE DEADLINE DATES

CONSEQUENCES OF DELAYED RESPONSE

Companies lose business because customers may want to make quick buying decisions.

A golden opportunity may be passed up because of time deadlines.

Customers start to doubt the efficiency of a company.

Employees apologize to customers and colleagues for their actions.

Excuses for the delayed response may sound insincere to a client.

Customers may question company priorities.

Workers must defend their responses by making excuses to co-workers and customers.

Customers may demand justification for a long drawn-out response from a company.

People get off schedule and projects are slowed down because of slow responses.

Projects get postponed because of long delays to complete a plan.

EXAMPLES OF LACK OF ACTION RESPONSE

A principal promised that teachers in each classroom would have a computer at the school. Several teachers had not received computers for their classrooms and they addressed their concerns to the principal. The principal's response was, "Let me check on that." The principal took no action and the teachers did not receive a computer that year.

An outstanding student asked her professor to write a letter of recommendation to apply for medical school. The professor promised to complete the letter of recommendation by the deadline date. She found out that the letter of recommendation was never received from the professor.

Two colleagues were discussing job opportunities in their field. One colleague told her co-worker she was hoping to obtain an interview and asked her to complete a reference form. The co-worker responded, "I'll be happy to do it for you." Once the colleague left the room, the co-worker threw the reference form in the trash can and never had any intention of sending it.

A customer buys a product with a customer guarantee satisfaction. The customer returns the product to receive a full refund. The company manager tells the customer that she will receive a refund in the mail in four to six weeks. The customer never received the refund in the mail.

TYPES OF LACK
OF ACTION RESPONSE

TELLING SOMEONE YOU WILL DO SOMETHING AND NOT CARRYING THROUGH ON YOUR WORD

NEVER HAVING ANY INTENTION TO SEND A REFUND THAT WAS PROMISED

VERBALLY MAKING AN AGREEMENT AND REFUSING TO FULFILL THE AGREEMENT

MAKING A FALSE PROMISE TO SOMEONE

MISLEADING SOMEONE BY ASSURING THE PERSON THAT HE OR SHE CAN DEPEND ON YOU

BEING UNTRUE TO YOUR COMMITMENTS

GIVING INACCURATE INFORMATION TO SOMEONE WHO RESPECTS YOU

NOT MAKING A GOOD FAITH ATTEMPT TO FOLLOW UP ON A REQUEST

MAKING A FUTURE AGREEMENT AND NOT LIVING UP TO IT

NOT FULFILLING AN OBLIGATION TO SOMEONE

CONSEQUENCES OF LACK OF ACTION RESPONSE

Individuals will not trust the professional.

Professional friendships can be hurt and damaged.

The professional is viewed as unreliable.

The negative image presented by the professional is reflected on the corporation.

Business relationships can be dissolved and discontinued by the lack of action.

The professional's reputation is doubted.

The professional may be representing him or herself in a lie.

The professional's good word is questioned.

The professional's lack of action makes other people look bad.

EXAMPLES OF INCORRECT RESPONSE

A patient requests a letter from her doctor's office to be faxed to an insurance company. The letter requested was to verify she had a medical procedure on a specific date. The doctor's office faxed several pages of the patient's confidential medical file instead of the specific letter the patient had requested. The patient's refund was delayed by several months.

A teacher requested his teaching evaluation be sent to a prospective employer. An inefficient secretary attaches his evaluation form to that of another teacher's evaluation. The committee reading the evaluation report does not realize the mistake as they review the document.

A company makes promises to a writer that the published book will circulate and remain in print for ten years. The writer inquires why the book has not been selling. He finds out the company has been sold and the new owners are not interested in publishing and reprinting his book. The rules of the company changed, but the writer was not informed of the new publication policies and correct guidelines.

A contestant enters a contest and does not realize that the third page of the application form was missing. The contestant is marked down by the judges for not completing the application.

TYPES OF INCORRECT RESPONSES

FAXING ADDITIONAL INFORMATION THAT WAS NOT REQUESTED

SENDING OUT CONFIDENTIAL INFORMATION BY MISTAKE

MISHANDLING IMPORTANT DOCUMENTS

MAILING INFORMATION TO THE WRONG PERSON

NOT NOTIFYING PEOPLE OF MAJOR COMPANY CHANGES

OUTDATED INFORMATION IS GIVEN TO CLIENTS

SENDING CHECKS AND FINANCIAL INFORMATION TO THE WRONG PARTY

INACCURATE INFORMATION IS SENT OUT ON CONTEST RULES

JOB DESCRIPTIONS POSTED IN AN OFFICE ARE NOT UPDATED AS POSITION REQUIREMENTS CHANGE

CONSEQUENCES OF INCORRECT RESPONSE

A client may prepare a report with outdated and incorrect information that must be revised and updated.

A customer's money or refund may be delayed for several months or a year.

Professionals can make customers very angry by mishandling information.

Professionals can lose contracts by sending incorrect items.

Items get misplaced into the hands of unscrupulous individuals.

Miscommunication can occur between companies over changes in policies.

A customer's reputation may be put on the line from the incorrect information.

A job applicant could lose a chance to be considered for a promotion or job transfer.

A professional could waste hours working on a project with irrelevant information.

A company may be threatened or sued for providing inaccurate and incorrect information to consumers.

EXAMPLES OF APPROPRIATE RESPONSE

A senior salesperson received a phone call from a colleague with a request to conduct a technology seminar. The salesperson returned the call before the end of the workday and agreed to conduct the seminar. A tentative agenda was sent the following day.

A professor received a grant application to write an extensive proposal from a colleague. The professor did not feel knowledgeable in the area of the proposed grant. A note was attached to the grant application and returned it to the colleague's mail box for review.

A team of executives working on a project received information from a contractor that there were difficulties working in the proposed time frame of the project. The team decided to address the difficulties by obtaining the specific problem areas identified by the contractor, reviewing their initial goals of the project, and rewriting a specific action plan and time line to address the new concerns.

A customer calls a company requesting a refund on defective merchandise. The company representative responds to the request by immediately faxing the guidelines for refunds to the customers. The representative also writes a personal note to the customer and lets him know that the company will try to correct the problem to his satisfaction.

TYPES OF
APPROPRIATE RESPONSE

ANSWERING MESSAGES WITHIN A REASONABLE TIME FRAME AS IN A 24-48 HOUR PERIOD

RELAYING MESSAGES TO THE PROPER PERSON

PROVIDING SUITABLE INFORMATION WHEN REQUESTED

GIVING CONSIDERATION TO REQUESTS AND INVITATIONS

CLARIFYING COMPLAINTS, PROJECTS AND DOCUMENTS

KEEPING UP WITH THE PACE OF PROJECTS

SCHEDULING REQUESTS FOR MEETINGS AND COMMITTEES TO EFFECTIVELY REACH PROJECT GOALS

ADDRESSING AGENDA ITEMS AND SIMPLE TASKS WITHIN REASONABLE PERIODS OF TIME

FINISHING PROJECTS AND REQUESTS THAT ARE COMMITTED TO BY A PROFESSIONAL

CONSEQUENCES OF APPROPRIATE RESPONSES

Customers and clients appreciate the professional's response to their needs.

Professionals show the customers that they value their business.

Teamwork runs smooth and efficient because professionals respond appropriately to each other's requests.

Professionals can meet time deadlines on projects more efficiently.

Professionals get a positive reputation that is respected among colleagues.

Professionals show others that they care about people's concerns and questions.

A more positive image is reflected for the corporation from the professional's actions.

Professional friendships have a much greater chance of continuing for long periods of time.

There is less conflict in the work setting because professionals are not making excuses about their responses.

CHAPTER 3

TIME CHOICES

Professionals make many choices during a workday that are directly related to the use of time. Since so much information is dated, time becomes an important element in the protocol of the workday. The use of time communicates a variety of messages to people and how they are viewed and respected by the professional. Professionals sometimes make too many time related choices that are problem areas in the work environment. These two time-related choices are as follows:

The professional uses time informally in formal settings.

The professional uses casual time in urgent situations.

These two problem areas will be discussed later in this chapter.

THE ESSENTIAL VALUE OF TIME

The element of time has an impact on the lives of people in their professional and personal world. Time is essential because it:

permits people to finish tasks so they feel good about their accomplishments

allows professionals to work on establishing life goals

provides people energy to have personal hobbies and interests

gives professionals space to cultivate and enrich their relationships with other people

lets people enjoy their family life

gives people opportunities to socialize and meet new friends

leaves room for professionals to take risks and meet new challenges

it lets people acknowledge their personal attributes and reevaluate their strengths and weaknesses

WHY TIME DATED INFORMATION IS IMPORTANT

Time dated information may help justify when something was mailed, emailed, texted or received by another company.

Time dated information may be needed to justify the professional's actions.

Time dated information shows that deadline dates were met on schedule.

Time dated information may justify when payments were made to a company or organization.

Time dated information provides others with a sense of the professional's efficiency in the work environment.

Time dated information reveals knowledge about the habits of the professional.

Time dated information can show if the professional has a caring or selfish attitude.

TIME DATED INFORMATION

The following is a list of items that can be dated or have time information included on them:

LETTERS AND CARDS

POSTAGE ON MAIL

FACSMILE

ANSWER MACHINE MESSAGES

MAIL OR ELECTRONIC RECEIPTS

CANCELLED CHECKS

EMAIL MESSAGES

TEXT MESSAGES

DOCUMENT DATES

PLANNERS AND ORGANIZERS

DATE BOOKS

YEARLY CALENDARS

WHY PROFESSIONALS NEED TIME DATED INFORMATION

to make future plans

to organize classes, committees and seminars

to develop a yearly calendar

to finish a project within a time limit

to organize a company party or social event

to make employee placements in a formalized schedule

to have a system that works effectively for numerous employees

to keep equipment and machines functioning properly

to maintenance equipment at regular intervals so that major breakdowns do not occur in a company

EXAMPLES OF USING INFORMAL TIME IN FORMAL SETTINGS

Professionals sometimes use time in an informal way for a formal setting.

A doctor with an office full of sick patients leaves them waiting for two hours while he is on the telephone making his personal stock trades.

A sales representative casually walks into a school drinking his coffee fifteen minutes late to make a presentation to teachers who need to get to class and plan for the day's activities.

A writer leaves a message on the answering machine for his editor to return his call on Wednesday. The editor travels for weeks at a time and is unsure which Wednesday the writer is referring to in his message.

A recent college graduate mails an undated letter to a corporation applying for a job. The secretary puts it in a file of undated material and it is not reviewed with the other applications.

A department chairperson leaves an office full of college students waiting outside for an hour while she is telling jokes with her colleagues.

CONSEQUENCES OF USING INFORMAL TIME IN FORMAL SETTINGS

Customers do not feel important or cared for by the professional.

It reflects a poor image on the professional and the company that he or she is representing to the audience.

It may show a lack of detail to time related matters.

Professionals may be showing weaknesses in their organization skills related to time.

Professionals are showing a lack of respect for colleagues and individuals waiting to see them in the work setting.

It is an example of how a company might handle a more serious matter.

It gives the impression that a company handles less important matters and cases.

WAYS PROFESSIONALS CAN EXPRESS TIME USE IN FORMAL SETTINGS

Professionals can verbally express and address some of the issues related to time in informal and formal settings. The customers want to know when the professional will be waiting on them or addressing their concerns.

"I will be with you in a few minutes."

"Please have a seat, you are the next appointment."

"The meeting will be over shortly and then we can visit."

"I will answer your phone message at my earliest convenience."

"Please forgive my oversight, I didn't see that you were waiting."

"If you do not mind waiting, I can talk with you in a couple of minutes."

EXAMPLES OF USING CASUAL TIME IN URGENT SITUATIONS

Professionals may act casual in situations that require an urgent response.

A department head left a request for funding application causally on her desk for three weeks. She suddenly asks a professor to write a major grant over the holiday weekend to meet the deadline.

A teacher casually arrives late for weekly teacher's meetings. He interrupts the guest speaker and makes a big scene upon his late arrival.

A supervisor gives out work assignments to the employees each week in a casual exchange. She does not indicate when the assignments are due. The supervisor is getting upset because employees are wasting time finishing their work.

A corporation has a busy schedule with many meetings and seminars. Employees are not showing up for important meetings and skipping the seminars. The supervisor addresses this concern with employees and they claim they did not know when the meetings were scheduled.

CONSEQUENCES OF USING CAUSAL TIME IN URGENT SITUATIONS

Items are sometimes misplaced because the professional is in no hurry to address them.

A professional looks as if he or she lacks organizational skills.

Colleagues may view the professional as lacking time management skills.

Important documents get lost because employees do not see the urgency to respond to them carefully.

Employees can cover up their inefficiency and poor work habits by blaming their employers for not telling them exact details or providing them with a schedule.

Documents that need careful handling are sometimes lost because they are not prioritized.

Sales opportunities could be lost because a casual approach is taken to respond to the client's needs.

Co-workers feel stress because urgent situations are taken for granted by the professional.

WAYS PROFESSIONALS CAN EXPRESS URGENT TIME CHOICES

Professionals can verbalize many statements that reflect an urgency of time. The following list illustrates some urgent time statements:

"I only have until Friday to make a decision."

"I am under a tight deadline and I need the information by the end of the week."

"The reports are needed by Wednesday so that corrections can be made on the final draft."

"The latest time to receive the documents is the last day of the month."

"The application cut off date is July 14, 2015."

"There will be no extensions on the deadline for the grant proposals."

"Weekly lesson plans are due every Friday in the principal's office."

"All projects must be finished a week before the conference date."

CHAPTER 4

HUMAN RELATIONS CHOICES

Many of the problems in the work environment are directly related to the human relations skills of the professionals. Professionals breaking the confidentiality of their colleagues can ruin good working relations. Disrespect for other human beings in the work place can create distrust and poor work habits. These problems are often created by a general lack of regard and caring for other people. Priorities in the work environment get out of focus. Workers sometimes get more concerned with their own selfish desires and ambitions that they become discourtesy and pay little attention to the needs of other workers. Rude remarks and impolite behaviors become so commonplace in some work environments that workers do not realize they are being disrespectful to others. The basic human relation choices in this area that are discussed in this chapter include:

CONFIDENTIALITY
Professionals showing regard for the private matters and concerns of others at work.

RESPECT
Professionals treating others with high regard, worth and consideration in work settings.

ATTITUDE
Professionals showing concern for the feelings and opinions of others in the work place.

MOTIVATION
Professionals who make a sincere effort to establish goals and accomplish tasks in the work arena.

EXAMPLES OF PROFESSIONALS BREAKING CONFIDENTIALITY

A secretary has access to privileged information on an employee's personal problems and she gossips it to other colleagues in the office.

A worker nearing retirement age requests information on retirement benefits. A colleague overhears her conversation and runs to the supervisor requesting her position before she announces her retirement.

An administrative assistant types teacher evaluations and professional reports. He makes copies of them and secretly shares them with office co-workers.

A professional shares with a trusted colleague that she is on a job search to obtain a promotion. The professional has not secured a position but her colleagues are already looking for her replacement.

A frustrated worker tells a co-worker, "I'm not sure how much longer I will be here if things do not change." The co-worker runs to the boss and tells him that the worker is going to quit her job.

CONSEQUENCES OF BREAKING CONFIDENTIALITY

Work relationships become stressed between employees.

A lack of trust develops in the work environment.

Information is passed to colleagues before it is finalized.

Personal employee information may become public knowledge in the workplace.

Incorrect information may be passed because false assumptions are made.

Employees may be hurt emotionally from an experience when someone breaks confidentiality.

Mistakes may occur because the confidential information is misinterpreted.

Employees start to spend too much work time gossiping about other employees.

WAYS PROFESSIONALS CAN SHOW CONSIDERATION FOR CONFIDENTIALITY

Professionals should respect people's personal information.

Professionals should be careful of idle chatter.

Professionals should not relate or pass information before it is finalized.

Professionals should show consideration by avoiding useless gossip.

Professionals should realize that information and circumstances might be in a changing state.

Professionals should be careful to not make assumptions about future occurrences.

Professionals need to use caution when making predictions about their colleague's future plans.

Professionals should respect privileged information of employees and colleagues.

EXAMPLES OF PROFESSIONALS SHOWING DISRESPECT

An employee creates funny and degrading pictures of employees on his computer. He prints up the pictures and passes them around the office to make fun of workers.

Two workers share a small cubicle at work. One worker makes personal calls and talks on the phone all day. The other worker has trouble concentrating on his work because of this irritating habit.

One employee goes through a co-worker's desk and uses her personal items while she is on an out-of-town job assignment.

A co-worker borrows a professional's reference book and does not return it for weeks at a time. The professional is always searching for the reference book to complete important assignments.

A colleague never brings enough lunch money and is always asking to borrow a few dollars for lunch. The colleague never pays the co-workers back and puts them in an uncomfortable situation.

CONSEQUENCES OF SHOWING DISRESPECT

Work relationships can be permanently damaged among co-workers.

Colleagues may become revengeful and angry with one another.

Professionals may feel vindictive toward each other.

Work production may become hampered by hurtful personal relationships.

A poor working environment may develop and project a less than positive company image.

Projects get delayed because employees are spending too much time on personal problems.

A corporation may lose good workers who go to other companies for a more positive work experience.

WAYS PROFESSIONALS CAN SHOW RESPECT TO OTHERS

Professionals should seek to build the confidence of others with positive statements.

Professionals should avoid cut downs that damage the self-esteem of employees, customers and co-workers.

Professionals should show consideration for other's use of time in work settings.

Professionals should seek to build confident relationships in the work environment.

Professionals should try not to antagonize or create useless disagreements.

Professionals should avoid annoying workers with irritating habits.

Professionals should try not to intentionally provoke colleagues to anger.

Professionals should show honor by caring for other individuals in the work environment.

EXAMPLES OF POOR ATTITUDES BY PROFESSIONALS

Professionals can show a bias and one-sided point of view. The following examples illustrate a bias and one-sided point of view:

"You will never get the job because you're not qualified."

"She will get the position because she knows the right person."

Professionals who demand their way without regard for the feelings and opinions of others.

During a high stress project an employee tells her colleagues, "I don't need your help. I can do it myself." The next step of the project consists of more team players assigned to work with her.

A sales representative wins a national sales contest but his ego gets the best of him. He downgrades his competition by personally attacking and making negative remarks about each one of them.

A husband and his wife in a dual career marriage and home business decide to go to movie for recreation. They argue about which movie to see and the wife gives in to her husband's choice. They go to the husband's movie choice and he is inconsiderate of his partner's feelings.

CONSEQUENCES OF SHOWING POOR ATTITUDES

A team effort may be hindered or sidelined by poor attitudes.

Office rapport and morale will probably be low and discouraging.

Professionals with bad attitudes may meet challenges with opposition.

Professionals may not want to work with someone who has a poor attitude.

A bad attitude by a professional may cause other employees to be less motivated.

Professionals may be unwilling to help and do favors for co-workers.

The professional in an office may become discouraged by his or her poor attitude.

Future business opportunities could be limited because of a professional's bad attitude.

WAYS PROFESSIONALS CAN SHOW POSITIVE ATTITUDES

Give other professionals a chance to prove themselves instead of making pre-judgements.

Listen to co-workers ideas as plans are being made.

Be accepting of different insights by other professionals.

Exchange different viewpoints and opinions without harsh judgements.

Give everyone on a team the chance to contribute thoughts and ideas.

Make sure opinions are shared before a final decision is reached.

Try to understand the point of view the person has from his or her personal situation.

Give credit and praise to acknowledge ideas shared by other colleagues.

EXAMPLES OF PROFESSIONALS WHO LACK MOTIVATION

A social service caseworker abuses company breaks and lunch periods. He often comes back late from lunch and takes a thirty-minute break rather than a fifteen-minute break each afternoon.

A group of teachers at an elementary school need to submit a monthly newsletter from their grade level. The teachers in first grade always prepare a small newsletter that is submitted after the deadline date. The principal is aware that this group of teachers does a very minimum amount of work.

A custodian has a special place he hides out during the day so office workers will not find him. He does this to avoid getting work requests from the office workers. The supervisor for the office must constantly page him to request his help with regular cleaning duties.

A professional does not like her job and would like to quit if she could afford it. She needs the money the job pays her, but she calls in sick almost every Friday so that she can party all weekend.

A grant writer finishes his work quickly and sneaks off from work thirty minutes early each day. The supervisor reviews his proposal and finds it is full of errors. The proposal has so many mistakes that the supervisor returns it to him to make corrections.

CONSEQUENCES OF SHOWING A LACK OF MOTIVATION

Professionals give the impression that they are not helping to reach company goals.

People do not believe that the professional takes his or her work seriously.

Professionals may be projecting to their employers that they are not showing team spirit.

Professionals may project an image that they take their positions for granted.

The work production level of the employee may be low because of his or her lack of motivation.

It shows the employee will not put in any extra effort to make projects and programs work.

The company or corporation may lose business to a more motivated company.

Professionals could lose opportunities for promotions and advancements because they are not motivated in their work.

WAYS PROFESSIONALS CAN SHOW MOTIVATION

Professionals can suggest new ideas to increase company productivity.

Professionals can show motivation by doing their fair share of the work.

Professionals can be positive examples and role models for less experienced employees.

Professionals can motivate company changes by making constructive contributions to an organization.

Professionals can motivate others by leading a group of people to accomplish a task.

Professionals can show their motivation through extra efforts reaching the company goals.

Professionals can exhibit motivation by organizing activities and events.

Professionals can use motivation to be supportive of other team members.

CHAPTER 5

COMPLETION CHOICES

Active professionals involved in a number of projects realize that there comes a point where these projects need to be completed or finished. Most professionals probably do not like to see projects linger for a long period of time. However, professionals have been in situations where the project or activity just sort of faded out of the picture. The professional may have been left wondering how the activity really turned out or what new approach to take on the next step of a project. The professional starts having doubts about his or her relationship with particular individual or company. A curiosity develops on how these uncompleted projects and left over cases should be processed or closed. There are several types of completion choices:

GRATITUDE CHOICES
The way professionals simply show a sincere appreciation to others for their kindness and fairness.

CLOSURE CHOICES
The way professionals follow through to end, close and finish projects or activities they have started with others.

PERSONAL GROWTH CHOICES
The way professionals seek to develop and increase personal awareness and satisfaction.

EXAMPLES OF
POOR GRATITUDE CHOICES

A school gives a baby shower for the principal. The principal mails out the thank you notes a year later after many of the teachers and staff have left the school.

A high school teacher spends sixty hours over his winter holiday break ordering books and supplies from the school budget. The teacher returns to school and shows the principal his work and hard efforts. The principal criticizes a typo in the teacher's report and shows no gratitude for his work.

A doctor's clinic is full of patients with an exceptionally busy schedule. A nurse volunteers to work her lunch hour to relieve some of the stress. The office manager and doctor forget to thank her for the extra time put in at work.

A sales executive constantly borrows audio-visual equipment from other staff members to make his own presentations look good. He is very slow to return the equipment and does not show appreciation to the person loaning him the equipment.

A parent has taken an active role in volunteering and leading a youth group. The director of the youth organization does not recognize outstanding parent leaders during an appreciation night.

CONSEQUENCES OF POOR GRATITUDE CHOICES

People assume the professional does not really care about them.

The professional develops a bad rapport with clients and customers.

It may make the professional look self-centered and unappreciative.

The professional may look as if he or she does not manage time well enough to show gratitude.

The professional may project an image that he or she has selfish desires and ambitions.

It shows that the professional is not thoughtful enough to take a minute to say thank you.

The inconsiderate behavior of the professional could be looked on negatively by colleagues.

The professional may look greedy or power hungry by others in the organization.

WAYS PROFESSIONALS CAN SHOW POSITIVE GRATITUDE

The professional can respond to the favor or act of kindness promptly.

The professional should in some way acknowledge the kind action or favor.

The professional should not be selective of rank or position when showing appreciation to others.

The professional should seek to recognize the extra effort of colleagues and employees.

The professional should not forget the small acts of kindness that often go unnoticed.

The professional can give positive strokes to others by verbally praising their actions.

The professional can respond to acts of kindness in a variety of ways such as thank you notes, warm words, cards and gifts.

The professional can volunteer to be of assistance to someone or do something kind for someone to show appreciation.

EXAMPLES OF
POOR CLOSURE CHOICES

A guest speaker arrives at a major conference and presents an outstanding lecture on a college campus. Campus officials overlook sending the speaker her honorarium.

A job applicant is invited to an out of state interview with a major corporation. The personnel department told the applicant that all expenses would be covered. The job applicant never received the travel expense check and has called the corporation three times to request the check.

A teacher purchases required educational materials with his supervisor's approval. The teacher provides receipts of his expenditures to the supervisor. The supervisor has a tight budget and decides that she can no longer reimburse the teacher. The teacher is left out in the cold and must absorb the loss.

A landscaping company tries to project an image of cleanliness in its advertisements. Workers finish a job and the workers leave behind trash, paper cups and soda bottles in a mess for the homeowner to clean.

CONSEQUENCES OF POOR CLOSURE CHOICES

People in organizations will doubt a person's word or professionalism.

It reflects a very poor public image on the association, organization or corporation.

A professional may be jeopardizing future career opportunities by his or her actions.

A professional may be looked at as being irresponsible.

The professional can be viewed as being a weak leader.

The group of professionals may not be seen as team players in a company.

The professionals may be viewed as not taking a stand on issues.

The corporate image is one that does not complete or finish assigned projects.

WAYS PROFESSIONALS CAN MAKE POSITIVE CLOSURE CHOICES

Live up to final promises and obligations made to an organization or company.

Make sure reimbursements are mailed to individuals and companies in a timely manner.

Write a letter to those affiliated with an organization explaining new policies or guidelines.

Conduct a meeting to address concerns and issues of a company before departing a position.

Complete all responsibilities and paperwork when leaving an elected office in an organization.

Follow up on last minute requests before leaving a position.

Finalize projects with a summary letter or final report.

Make a folder of important information to pass on to the next professional who takes the position.

EXAMPLES OF POOR PERSONAL GROWTH CHOICES

Corporate executives are debating a major project. A professional executive storms out of the office angry about the final decision.

A committee is experiencing harsh feelings during monthly meetings. There are heated discussions and one committee member is discouraged. She does not discuss the problem with anyone and resigns from the committee.

A professional notices that two of his colleagues are bickering about the work situation. He does not talk with either of them about their bad feelings. He ignores the problem hoping it will go away.

A teacher has a difficult student in class who has caused a major disturbance. The teacher gets upset and reacts by yelling at the student.

A day care worker has a two-year-old student who gets mad and kicks the wall. The worker responds angrily by calling the child's mom and sending the child home.

A nurse does not finish her final reports at the shift change. She tries to put her work and responsibilities off on the nurses who arrive for the next shift. The nurse has the attitude that she is not responsible for writing the reports. She feels that she is a nurse, not a writer.

CONSEQUENCES OF POOR PERSONAL GROWTH CHOICES

A professional may become discouraged by his or her lack of progress.

Friendships can be damaged if professionals are negative to each other.

A professional may lose direction of career goals.

A professional may become disorganized in completing job tasks.

The personal relationships of the professional can be stifled by lack of planning.

The professional may face opposition with a lack of self-confidence.

The professional may lose sight of the important things in life.

The professional may experience confusion and bewilderment about the end results that he or she wants to achieve.

WAYS PROFESSIONALS CAN GAIN PERSONAL GROWTH

The professional can react calmly in stress situations.

The professional can listen to people who express problems and concerns.

The professional can make helpful suggestions to people in need of help.

The professional can work out an action plan with other employees to address problem areas.

The professional can make a list of goals he or she wants to personally accomplish in life.

The professional can prioritize needs and desires on a rotating basis.

The professional has the opportunity to manage and organize time to meet personal goals.

The professional can seek help and obtain advisement from friends and colleagues.

CHAPTER 6

PRINCIPLES OF HUMAN RELATIONS PROTOCOL

There are some basic principles that embody the ideas of the human relations protocol. Professionals may choose to consider ways that they can develop a foundation using these human relations skills. The principles of the human relations protocol discussed in this chapter include:

ACKNOWLEDGMENT
GENEROSITY
SINCERITY
CARING
GOODWILL
CONTRIBUTIONS
CONFIDENCE
PEACEMAKING
COOPERATION
ACCEPTANCE
ASSURANCE
CONSCIENTIOUS
ACCOUNTABILITY
AFFIRMATION
INITIATIVE

HUMAN RELATIONS PROTOCOL

PRINCIPLE #1

ACKNOWLEDGMENT

◆

The professional should seek to acknowledge people who are in close proximity in work situations.

WAYS PROFESSIONALS CAN SHOW ACKNOWLEDGMENT

Handshake

Oral Greeting

Smile

Head Nodding

Show Interest

Pat on Shoulder

Pick Up a Dropped Item

Give Directions

Offer Help

HUMAN RELATIONS PROTOCOL

PRINCIPLE #2

GENEROSITY

◆

The professional should exhibit generosity toward people
in the work setting.

WAYS PROFESSIONALS CAN SHOW GENEROSITY

Sharing Advice

Giving Suggestions

Distributing Information

Imparting Advice

Furnishing Guidance

Dispensing Guidelines

Giving Hints

Making Recommendations

HUMAN RELATIONS PROTOCOL

PRINCIPLE #3

SINCERITY

◆

The professional should seek to be sincere in his or her actions in the work environment.

WAYS PROFESSIONALS CAN SHOW SINCERITY

Being Genuine With Ideas

Being Trustworthy With Information

Being Honorable in Actions

Being Truthful About Incidents

Being Faithful to a Cause

Being Fair in Activities

Being Frank about Mistakes

Being Open about Problems

HUMAN RELATIONS PROTOCOL

PRINCIPLE #4

CARING

◆

The professional should seek to be caring
about others in the workplace.

WAYS PROFESSIONALS CAN SHOW CARING

Show Attention to Those in Need

Give Condolence to Those in Pain

Being Watchful to Prevent Accidents

Empathize With Difficult Situations

Recognize the Suffering of Others

Being Concerned About Problems

Give Support to Those Having Trouble

Being Sympathetic to People's Feelings

HUMAN RELATIONS PROTOCOL

PRINCIPLE #5

GOODWILL

◆

The professional should show goodwill toward
others in the working community.

WAYS PROFESSIONALS CAN SHOW GOODWILL

Being Supportive of Professionals in
Problem Relationships

Being Charitable to a Good Cause

Having a Gentle Spirit toward Those in Needy Situations

Showing Encouragement to Other Professionals

Unselfishly Giving Time to Improve a Situation

Serving Others Who Want to Better Their Conditions

HUMAN RELATIONS PROTOCOL

PRINCIPLE #6

CONTRIBUTIONS

◆

The professional should seek to make valuable
contributions to the work environment.

WAYS PROFESSIONALS CAN SHOW CONTRIBUTIONS

Participating in Work Projects with a Positive Attitude

Furnishing New Ideas for Company Improvements

Sharing Concerns about Anticipated Business Problems

Making Suggestions to Improve Company Efficiency

Developing a Plan to Address a Problem Area

Forming New Goals to Reach Higher Expectations

HUMAN RELATIONS PROTOCOL

PRINCIPLE #7

CONFIDENCE

◆

The professional should seek to be confident about
his or her skills in the work setting.

WAYS PROFESSIONALS CAN SHOW CONFIDENCE

Know Your Department's Expectations

Be Familiar with Company Regulations

Update Skills as Company Needs Change

Meet People Outside of One Specialized Areas

Interact Informally at Company Social Functions

Be Ready and on Time for Department and Staff Meetings

HUMAN RELATIONS PROTOCOL

PRINCIPLE #8

PEACEMAKING

◆

The professional should seek to be a peacemaker during
tense situations in the workplace.

WAYS PROFESSIONALS CAN SHOW PEACEMAKING

Exhibit a Good Attitude in a Difficult Situation

Encourage a Co-Worker to Cool Off

Offer Suggestions for a Compromise

Apologize for Hurting Someone

Settle a Quarrel

Talk Over a Disagreement at a Later Time

Try Not to Over React to a Difficult Person

HUMAN RELATIONS PROTOCOL

PRINCIPLE #9

COOPERATION

◆

The professional should seek to show cooperation
to co-workers during daily work tasks.

WAYS PROFESSIONALS CAN SHOW COOPERATION

Encourage Someone to Take on a New Challenge

Work Together to Improve a Situation

Contribute Time to Company Planning

Do a Fair Share of Work When Involved in Teams

Participate in Joint Projects

Relieve a Co-Worker who is Stressed Out

Befriend a New Employee

HUMAN RELATIONS PROTOCOL

PRINCIPLE #10

ACCEPTANCE

◆

The professional should seek to show acceptance to people
who have different beliefs or ideas from his or her
own belief system.

WAYS PROFESSIONALS CAN SHOW ACCEPTANCE

Welcome Unique Points of View

Consider Cultural Backgrounds of Individuals

Accentuate Agreeable Points in a Conversation

Find Similarities among Different Cultures

Draw on Other People's Experiences

Consider a Variety of Opinions When Making Decisions

Listen Attentively to People's Concerns

HUMAN RELATIONS PROTOCOL

PRINCIPLE #11

ASSURANCE

◆

The professional should feel assurance about his or her skills and abilities in the workplace.

WAYS PROFESSIONALS CAN SHOW ASSURANCE

Maintains Hopeful Disposition When Facing Endeavors

Show a Determination to Complete Difficult Tasks

Bravely Confront Changes in the Workplace

Be Courageous in Trying New Things

Meet Challenges with an Optimistic Attitude

Remaining Calm during Upheavals in the Work
Environment

HUMAN RELATIONS PROTOCOL

PRINCIPLE #12

CONSCIENTIOUS

◆

The professional should seek to have a conscientious
attitude about his or her work.

WAYS PROFESSIONALS CAN SHOW CONSCIENTIOUSNESS

Being Responsible for Daily Tasks

Performing Job Duties Thoroughly

Fulfilling Work Obligations

Accurately Checking for Mistakes

Carrying Out Promises

Being Accountable for the End Product

Reviewing Reports for Errors

Explaining the Reasons Why Decisions are Made

HUMAN RELATIONS PROTOCOL

PRINCIPLE #13

ACCOUNTABILITY

◆

The professional should seek to be accountable for
his or her actions in the work setting.

WAYS PROFESSIONALS CAN SHOW ACCOUNTABILITY

Investigate the Details of a Situation
Before Making Comments

Research the Facts of a Case Thoroughly

Provide Studies to Back up Statements

Make Evaluations after a Thorough Investigation

Furnish information That Supports Opinions

Use Data to Support Judgments

HUMAN RELATIONS PROTOCOL

PRINCIPLE #14

AFFIRMATION

◆

The professional should maintain a positive affirmation about the mission and goals of the place he or she is working.

WAYS PROFESSIONALS CAN SHOW AFFIRMATION

Maintain a Supportive Attitude to Reach
Organizational Goals

Propose Steps for Reaching Company Goals

Help the Organization or Business Achieve Its Mission

Agree to Assist Projects That Benefit the
Whole Organization

Commit to Achieving a Common Purpose

Have Consideration for Items That Serve
Large Numbers of People

HUMAN RELATIONS PROTOCOL

PRINCIPLE #15

INITIATIVE

◆

The professional should seek to show initiative in
work activities and projects.

WAYS PROFESSIONALS CAN SHOW INITIATIVE

Institute a More Productive Plan

Start a Fresh Scheme

Originate a New Proposal

Take the First Step for Change

Put a Contemporary Approach in Place of an Old One

Give Suggestions for Revising a Project

Propose Brand New Guidelines

INDEX

U

Urgent situations, 29

V

Value (s), 8

W

Weak, 35
Weekly, 45
Whole organization, 95
Workplace, 82

Y

Yearly calendar (s), 32

AFTERWORD

After working twenty plus years in the professional world it has been difficult for me to remember some of those unprofessional mishaps. Those experiences of being shown disrespect, getting no or a delayed response from people and hearing professionals being inconsiderate of a person's confidentiality have all been hurtful to me as a professional and as a person. I was able to overcome these unprofessional mishaps by finding positive professionals who helped me believe in the goodwill and caring nature of people. If professionals use a human relations approach in the workplace that shows respect and goodwill toward others it can make the day to day work environment more positive and fulfilling for the working professional. *Human Relations Protocol* was written to encourage professionals to have a caring and cooperative spirit toward others in the work environment.

9 780996 800822